Luminosity

Inspirations for the Soul

Deepti Belliappa Ganapathy

Dedication

When you write for your soul, your core hears the voice.

I write for my heart, while my readers hear my whispers.

To everyone who understands Luminosity!

Contents

Preface

Luminosity means something that gives off light. It is the vibrance that brings the glow. It is the hope that one sees, as life goes through various stages of emotions. As per Buddhist teachings, Luminosity refers to the purest clarity of the mind, when it is free from any discriminating thoughts. To be in a state of luminosity, is to look at life from every facet and yet find your-self.

This book is a compilation of poems that paint every facet of luminosity in moments around us. As you delve into each line, you will experience a visual journey that will transport you to a divergent and extraordinary facet that weaves so many emotions into the tapestry of our lives. It radiates the brilliance that exists and the brightness in the smallest moments around us.

Acknowledgement

With love and thanks to my parents, brother, husband and children for their enduring patience and being a part of my life journey as I continue to grow as a person.

I am grateful to my professional community who has given me the confidence of seeing inspiration in everything around us and giving me my wings to ink from my heart. .

I am deeply grateful to my family and friends who have stood by me with their unwavering support and honest guidance always.

I acknowledge the support of the team at Notion Press publishing who has worked with me tirelessly to bring this book to its fruition.

Author Bio

Deepti Belliappa Ganapathy

Luminosity is Deepti's second poetry book. It is a collection of diverse poems that explore various emotions that are weaved into the fabric of life. Previously she has authored Equanimity (by Bookleaf Publishing), a compilation of poems as well as a children's book titled '366 words in Bengaluru' by FunOkPlease Publishing (Now Amar Chitra Katha). A Public Relations consultant by profession, Deepti finds her inspiration in her own journey and sees joy in little things.

A keeper of promises, with a smiling heart,
Nurturing relations from the start!
A cherished bearer of words every now and then,
A journey with insights enriched to pen.
Every equation has some charm for sure,
Much to learn far and near!
Life has much to offer for sure,
Live, love laugh is the only cure.

Tales of the Hushed Breeze

Tales of the hushed breeze I hear,
Its soft yet fluttering my soul but not in fear!
Did I hope for some unreal light to shine?
Or mysterious movements that are hard to define.

Tales of the hushed breeze have a different echo now,
The forsaken streets lit with dim lights somehow.
I looked around for the presence I hoped,
My heart yearned for the kindred spirits- a past which I coped.

Tales of the hushed breeze after seasons and years did pass,
But the kindred presence remains alas!
Return if possible my heart would pray,
While the world chants rest in peace every day!

Tales of the hushed breeze then speaks to me,
It was the voice of a loved one with an unfortunate destiny.
With a gentle breeze and calm I feel,
Comforting me to find solace and better heal.

Tales of the hushed breeze remind me of days,
When these little moments of chatter forever stays!
Now a story that I charter down memory lane,
Hoping to go back in time again!

Tales of the hushed breeze tell me in peace they see,
With no regrets, they hope to be forever free.
Not to hold them clinched with ache,
As they savour a better world free from heartbreak.

Tales of the hushed breeze with calm they share,
Gently reminding me of every care!
To look forward to every new journey ahead,
With optimism and hope, a fine spread.

Tales of the hushed breeze sing with cheer,
The leaves dance and tell me it's a different blessing dear.
Only I can hear these voices I know,
But it's not my insanity; instead the universe has a different show.

Tales of the hushed breeze now have eased to a gripping silence,
Almost a dream awakened, my life journey has new guidance.
Nothing is forgotten or lost in time,
It's like a new ring from bamboo to a metal bell wind chime.

Magical Euphony into the Night

In the still of the night, the calm is real,
In deep slumber, traveling through dreams, wound up in a curl!
Stories are many, of every vision that dawns on me,
This visual magical euphony into the night is a time capsule that
sets me free.

At the strike of twelve, the little girl celebrates with glee,
An imaginary cake being cut is an innocent magical euphony into
the night to see.
Family and friends with midnight wishes hope to be the first,
To wish and celebrate, the excitement is like a starburst.

The modest bride with the excited groom dance into the night,
A new beginning with mixed emotions is a complex sight.
Counting years or making moments count they say,
This magical euphony into the night has an unconditional play.

The melody of instruments that spontaneously radiate the night,
It's a music jam they say, around the bon fire so bright.
Every chord that is pitched with harmony, an auditory sight,
Strangers become friends; it's a perfect magical euphony into the
night.

Away from the city lights, as we rush to nature's haven,
Into the green forests, the paths are silent and unspoken.
As the stars decorate the skies with a grand sparkle,
Dancing fire flies is a magical euphony into the night; truly
unstoppable.

Have you wondered about the night flowers that bloom?
The moon flower or blue water lily brightens the gloom!
The chance sighting of the Queen of the Night,
This glowing magical euphony into the night is worth the sleep
fight.

Standing on a bridge, the picturesque magical euphony into the
night I see,
Is in the reflection of the moon and stars over water till eternity!
The moon glade has etched a canvas like no other,
The artist is a miracle with an art that is a worthy cover.

The everyday chaos has much to brave,
New challenges, it's a fight worth the save.
Pause that manic and let your heart listen and see,
It's not just in the day, but a miraculous magical euphony into the
night.

Fragmented Philosophy

Bearing a fragmented philosophy yet smiling ahead,
As I lay still, pondering over my past in bed.
To the world, keeping troubles at bay, we must smile,
An irony of life at every mile!

The struggles of the past are real and seen,
But how do I explain these fragmented philosophies, an unimaginable scene.
Equations that got lost in time,
Bring back tears, a painful rhyme.

Some lost lives as a twist of destiny,
Though we built dreams; imagining eternity.
In those fragmented philosophies were a few that chose to live a life apart,
Was it time, distance or just outlived the journey and now a broken heart.

The fragmented philosophies remind me for sure,
Be your own person that will be your only cheer.
Have that circle to call your own,
But be prepared to walk the journey all alone.

There are invisible scars for sure,
Holding me together, coping with every fear.
The world sees the façade of strength I know,
Inside I am a little girl with fragmented philosophies that grow.

Tunes of Pensive Moments

Navigating the bustling streets, along the dimmed lit road,
Almost a downpour, yellow alert it showed.
The radio played tunes of pensive moments of another time,
Indelible for sure, we rhapsodize in this retro chime.

Every beat had a soulful voice so pure,
Our own bickering or the traffic around silenced for sure.
Catapulted through time, magnifying the fabric of life,
Memories cascade our hearts; there was no time for strife.

The music is a turning point for that yearning soul,
A poignant reminder of a reflective life, as a whole!
The common perception is the sadness we connect,
With tunes of pensive moments we believe that's the effect.

Irony of this music, it's not limited to sadness,
Packed with lyrics or just instruments, echoing happiness!
Almost feeling understood, an assurance in its tune,
The tunes of pensive moments can be the perfect boon.

So keep that 'go to' playlist handy with you,
A mood lifter or the perfect companion, it's definitely true.
Validating our emotions, joy and sadness, heal us right,
Evoking that human experience thrives in a balanced fight.

Rising from Absolution

A lifetime gone by for some in remorse,
Looking back wondering in regret or worse!
Is it worthwhile to be wrapped in this guilt?
Rising from absolution a respite waiting to be built.

Choices are made, own them now,
Mistakes can be many, accept them somehow.
Rising from absolution will tread the way,
There is hope in this journey, but no room for delay.

Broken in ways, one would wonder,
Hoping the heart looks beyond this endless fluster.
The past and the future have a symphony set,
Rising from absolution will wipe away any room for regret.

No one said that this path was simple,
It remains filled with obstacles, definitely not nimble.
The heart hears the faint whispers along the way,
Rising from absolution forgiveness is set to play.

As you are rising from absolution, you are rewarded your time,
Ride the boat of humility and gratitude, the peace is sublime.
Step ahead towards the light of new beginnings here,
Bid adieu to the regret, welcome with cheer.

Quiescence of the Stars - A Mute Resolve

Gazing up at the night sky I see,
The soulful moon speaks to me.
She pours her heart with much hope,
The quiescence of the stars is hard for her to cope.

In a universe that is bustling with glittering cheer,
The quiescence of the stars is an unsettling fear.
Defying gravity as the universe creates a canvas so rare,
Every planetary object has a role to prepare.

The brightest star or the biggest there is,
Make a wish that one must not miss.
Just like humanity, stars have a life span that counts,
So the quiescence of the stars knows no bounds.

The same pattern keeps families as one,
But acrimonious equations create quiescence of the stars and that's
no pun.
Often a discord or a conceit driven silence we see,
Drifted apart, human equations often broken till eternity!

Together we rise, divided we fall,
Mankind must learn a mantra for all.
The quiescence of the stars must be unmuted for sure,
A dialogue will engage the heart and mind with cheer

Cinders of Optimism

The race against time is filled with hope,
Humanity has signed up for an ordeal hard to cope.
The cinders of optimism must be kept alive,
Effort will not be in vain if we strive.

The modern landscape has captured our sight,
As we yearn for the lush green with all our might.
Crowded cities yet green buildings thrive,
Cinders of optimism are balancing modernization to survive.

Connections have transpired from offline to online mode,
Emotions have become symbols and an alphabetic code.
Minds are now alone with every year gone by,
Cinders of optimism will glow, as communities fly high.

Play time without devices, basking in the sun,
A scene of another decade, our kids miss this pure fun.
Cinders of optimism radiate with simple picnics and games,
Short-lived to only get captured quickly for memories in social
media frames.

Concrete jungles are built by people with hearts,
Humanity has not disappeared in most parts.
Cinders of optimism will keep generations to revive the old,
Memories made will anchor the future for us to uphold.

Filament of Karma

As we untangle the filament of karma,
Each strand has a pact with life and eternity.
The cosmic aura that glows with pride,
It's a tapestry of many emotions that balances this ride.

Decades gone by, the social fabric has changed,
Some stay in the heart, while others are estranged.
Filament of karma might make an unforgettable knot,
Intertwined by emotions and trust, it's an unbreakable thought.

Choices to be made, the decision is done,
Soak in the consequence, its best for everyone.
The filament of karma, will support the weight of your choice,
It's no longer a crossroad, assured by my heart's voice.

The filament of karma, remain twined by my fate,
It's never an easy dance, the struggle will always resonate.
But the melody has an indelible symphony that echoes,
Reminding us of memories, with every moment it grows.

We often hope that the filament of karma hold strong,
As we go with the flow, hoping nothing can go wrong.
Challenge the path and hope to make that change,
But destiny overpowers and it's a reset on the life stage.

Decode - The Fading Emotion

A generation that struggles, so much is to be said,
It's a mind and heart that has it all stored in the head.
The language has changed and so has the emotion,
The fading emotion, it's a new sort of commotion.

Organic conversations are almost fading in our past,
Emotions are absent; they have been replaced by a graphical cast.
There is a slang that one must master to stay relevant,
The fading emotion, it's a struggle to remain pertinent.

The heartfelt conversation, with a touch that matters,
Devices have erased distances replaced by small chatters.
Technology has eased the distance and time bound concern,
The missed emotion, decoding, there is much to learn.

Geographies are many; languages are their only hope,
Messages being spread in myriad languages; much to cope!
The fading emotion, it's never the same,
The human framework, it's a complex game.

Words are many, so much to say,
Weave the fabric of hope and trust every day.
Humanity has much to unfold in this web of life,
Don't forget the fading emotion, stay free from strife.

Reflections of Infiniteness

Sitting on the yellow swing, overlooking the city,
With love in my heart, there are reflections of endlessness.
Surrounded by all, yet I hear my inner voice remind me,
Preserving what matters is a dance with destiny.

The heart promises to take the hand and care,
The mind teases with mindless anxiety that will scare.
Calm the spirit, I find myself baffled,
The reflections of infiniteness will tread the path less travelled.

The journey with many have been compelling and sure,
Promises made, but challenges are enveloped with fear.
The reflections of infiniteness were heard with each of them,
But this journey is mine, hence no one can condemn.

The sprawling green grass speaks with cheer,
Or the efflorescent flowers that colour the landscape here!
The calm water that paints my reflection amidst modernity,
Yet I hide in the grotto of life believing in reflections of infinity.

As I walk through life with dreams that matter,
The rules of this journey are my own with sadness or laughter.
Even if alone, the reflections of infiniteness will ring a memorable chime,
With pride I will march, as this is the melody of my own rhyme

Dazzling Silhouettes

In the still of the night, the sound of my footsteps was heard,
The lights were dim and my vision almost felt blurred.
The stillness of the night reminded me of being followed,
By kindred spirits or the dazzling silhouettes, it was a unique episode.

The void of the departed, an absence I felt so much,
That I yearned for their presence or hoped for that final touch!
The silence was broken with some background music I hear,
An odd scenario on this quaint street, seeing dazzling silhouettes cheer!

Looked around to find no one in sight,
Appalled that the dazzling silhouettes was ours that night!
Strange are the patterns of the mind and heart,
Are we imagining this symphony, a musical art?

In life the shadow represents all things dark,
It's unfortunate to narrow our vision so stark.
While we radiate the optimism with care,
The dazzling silhouettes though lively; are a negative fare.

Life has a mix of both they say,
The coordinated dazzling silhouettes will perfect the way.
The past wounds and fear wrapped in your shadow will cure,
Into the needed wisdom as an evolved self for sure!

The Bygone Treasure

Perched on the shelf in the attic it was placed,
A timeless box, so many memories in my mind raced.
As I opened the box with nostalgia and a warm heart,
I found the bygone treasure, a secret key to a treasured art.

With this key, I opened the chest of drawers,
Inside which were safely kept powers.
Journals of the time when wars had no voice,
The bygone treasure hid the untold truth from making any noise.

Every page was laced in loss and tears,
Of loved ones killed succumbed to unfortunate fears.
These were secrets of monstrosity and prejudiced times,
Guarded by the bygone treasure of heart wrenching rhymes!

Every word had depth that echoed with hope,
Battles that scarred the heart, struggling to cope!
The bygone treasure reminds us of people gone but not forgotten,
The changing seasons, from summer to autumn!

Tears rolled down my cheeks with each word, a poignant reminder
of this time gone by,
The true heroes were almost forgotten, now stars in the sky.

I wonder if they could be memorialised for their sacrifice and service for us,
The bygone treasure has opened the chest, finally sharing a history so proud, nothing to remain anonymous.

The Harmonious Calm

The daily grind, the chaos doesn't end,
It's a rollercoaster ride but a break we recommend.
Life is on fast forward, time to find the pause,
There is a harmonious calm to discover, so ignore the flaws.

There is music in the morning quiet,
The stillness is magical after an eventful night.
Utilise strength to traverse the cacophony of the day ahead,
It's a harmonious calm as you find ways to unplug instead.

The silence that holds our soul with hope,
Artistically captured in life's canvas, which we must cope!
Not just meditation or the yogi finds this purpose I know,
Looking within for the harmonious calm, it is your show.

The whisper of that promising intuition that leads the way,
The deepest reflections surface as inspiration is here to stay.
Creativity has found a solace in this retreat,
The harmonious calm reflects inner wisdom on the hot seat.

In Ubuntu we reflect on the power of unity,
I am because you are - etched in time as the only destiny.
The harmonious calm confides in me as my own,
The belonging to self and the universe is the quintessential zone.

Tittle Tattle All the Way

As I walked through the bustling streets,
The crowd was hard to manoeuvre powered by the loud beats.
Inspite of the congested path, I found my way,
But I soon noticed the tittle tattle all the way in the midst of the day.

At the onset it felt like tittle tattle to my ears,
The idle talk and rumours felt like a shield to their fears.
I imagine they hope to hide their own weakness may be,
The tittle tattle all the way felt like a blanket to keep them free.

There were stories that can grip your heart,
Pause your day and delay your goal chart.
Often far from the truth or a story stretched to delight,
The tittle tattle all the way is a burden on their conscience, it's a wasted fight.

A topic for many, I am bound to be spoken about,
In the tittle tattle all the way, there is no room for doubt.
But a clear heart and mind I move with pride,
With values so deep and karma is my guide.

It takes all kinds of people, to perfect this land,
Accept and accommodate is the best stand.
The tittle tattle all the way can envelope your being,
Staying connected to your centre is the best you will be seeing.

Ruptured Moments in Time

It feels like yesterday when we met,
There were memories that we spun together we set.
Decades later, I smile in gratitude for the times,
The ruptured moments in time present a nostalgic rhyme.

We have gone our own ways after all these years,
Now the ruptured moments in time, our friendship didn't brave the
storm of fears.
In hindsight our foundation seemed to be shaken with ease,
Or bound by time, our friendship did cease.

Looking back I remember the laughs and tears,
Grateful for memories and milestones over the years!
Heartfelt conversations that only your ears did hear,
In the ruptured moments of time, in sadness I shed this tear.

I am grateful for the learning I had with you,
I grew as a person inside out too.
The ruptured moments of time might erase the moments we shared,
Wishing you well in life, and hope you are forever cared.

In this journey, people come and go,
Some move on while others stand through high and low.
In the ruptured moments of time, I cherish this fabric of life,
There are no guarantees that it will be free of strife.

Chorus of the Songbirds

The bouquet of roses, the romantic gesture under the moonlit night,
A keepsake memory for that young love, a sweet sight!
Hearty dedications and surprise gifts that rule the lovers' code,
It's like the chorus of the Songbirds, a memorable hallmark episode.

It's truly picture perfect in this canvas of youth most see,
Captured moments, now a social media frenzy!
Swooned by the moment today for sure,
Like the chorus of the Songbirds, a melodious song to cheer.

Time has passed and much has changed now,
The same couple has a different picture somehow.
Comforting meals, a cup of coffee is a treat,
A new chorus of the Songbirds it's a mature heartbeat.

It's no longer dreamy for that beating heart,
Pragmatic and real, it's a valuable part.
Conversations that matter, it's a new kind of beautiful,
This chorus of the Songbirds is comforting and delightful.

For many, it appears like a color fade,
Don't mistake the color change, it's a cherished shade.
It takes years for many, a rare find,
This chorus of the Songbirds is the perfect kind.

Meandering Reflections

Standing in the room, I look around to see,
I see my reflection in the mirror, looking back at me.
I am being asked about the person I am today,
The meandering reflects the echoing of an elucidative life play.

There is a little girl, aching for little joys,
Meandering reflections illustrate that the smile is not always for toys.
Often forgotten, her biggest cheer is the gift of time,
Resulting in happiness from the heart which is truly sublime!

In these meandering reflections, I see the career woman,
Facing her battles, balancing life so uncertain!
Responsibilities are many; the job may be at stake,
Juggling many roles without notice, nothing to forsake!

In this maze I find my inner self gazing at me,
Asking me about the person I am or hope to be.
In these meandering reflections, I see the small moments here,
Beyond ambition and money, memories give me cheer.

Through the meandering reflections, I ponder about my heart,
Have I nurtured all equations and truly done my part.
Tomorrow when I see the greater force, question my being,
I want to look within with pride and like what I am seeing

Reminiscence of an Etched Memory

I flipped the pages of the years gone by,
Feels like yesterday, the reminiscence of an etched memory is hard
to deny.
The hearty laughter with timeless moments that were spent,
With the fusion of sorrow and tears from undeniable losses, a time
to vent!

These were captured in a frayed journal of a forgotten ancestor,
An artistic handwriting with scribbles that seem to add character;
The pages were shrivelled but the words did not fade,
With the reminiscence of an etched memory, their depth was hard
to evade.

There were stories of struggles with freedom and personal toil,
There were deep shades of racism and disparity, a true blood boil.
Voices of few that dared to be the change,
The reminiscence of an etched memory was an inspiration through
every outrage.

It was not all about a war cry or heroes of the land,
There was a mysterious love story, blossoming in this turmoil,
hard to understand.
The words were fragile but could not suppress the emotion at play,
It was a capture in the reminiscence of an etched memory that will
forever stay.

I caressed the book in my arms with a deep sigh,
Transported to another time, I will not deny.
The reminiscence of an etched memory, have given me reason to see,
The beauty and pure joy in a forgotten simplicity!

I want to be tangled in these woven threads of yesterday,
It seems like a mess that will lift my soul every day.
The reminiscence of an etched memory have given many reasons
to yearn for more,
Occupying my soul, deeper in its core

Grievance of the Distressed

The shrieking cries of the little pups in the rain,
Homeless and uncared for, they remain.
I made my way to rescue them from despair,
The grievance of the distressed pups is a complex repair.

There are many left untamed and uncared we see,
So much disparity between the pampered pets and the strays' destiny!
In little things and simple steals they find their peace,
The grievance of the distressed animals, find solace with ease.

In another scene, the child gazes at the pages in candle light,
With eyes so wide, amused at an otherwise ordinary but in his eyes a rare sight!
Under the seeping hut, dilapidated all around,
While his mother cooks with love in spite of the scary thunder sound.

Their torn clothes did not shield them from the cold,
Neither did the breaking hut truth be told.
It was their time, simple with cheer,
The grievance of these distressed emotions had no fear.

The seeming aches that grapple the world,
Without questions asked, fate surprises all that is hurled.
The grievance of the distressed echoes with an unbearable pain to cope,
It's time to delve into your core and shield it with hope.

Hushed Radiance

Gazing into the night sky I see,
Infinite possibilities that the universe holds for me!
I can hear the stars hushed radiance ever so pure,
Reminding me of a fulfilled journey, one must endure.

Every aspiration that shines through the sky,
Dreams are many, yearning to fly.
The time gone by reminds me to make every moment count,
The stars radiance softly speaks into my ear for this life I must account.

The radiance of the light coming through,
The luminosity of the stars is what we all knew.
The stars radiance softly speak about the celestial beauty on this life canvas we see,
The captivation of this aura in an emotional yet contemporary society is a guarantee.

Contentment and balance is our hope,
That's the beauty of life to cope.
The stars radiance murmur about a life mantra we yearn to ape,
As we sail into memories that propel our escape.

In nature we find the magic of life,
Deciphered with sweet blossoms, free from strife!
The stars hushed radiance guide my journey with ease,
Hindered by the human complications, always the biggest tease!

Momentary Resonance

Who has seen tomorrow, we all may say,
So why not live like this is your last day.
If life could be lived so fearlessly with cheer,
The momentary resonance of life will be free of fear.

Nothing is permanent, the life scroll shares,
The fleeting moment passes by, that's what scares.
An almost a lifetime like relationship it may seem,
But the momentary resonance, wipes away in a second like a bad dream.

Death comes like a shadow, with no reason to prepare,
The looming fear of uncertainty has no room to beware.
The momentary resonance can spoil the life we lead,
Every second well lived is all we need.

Everything is transitory, known to us,
That little insect buzzing around without a fuss,
The momentary resonance of a life no more tomorrow it has seen,
But doesn't stop living with glamor and sheen.

Every being is shaded in the same gradient we know,
The momentary resonance is a universal show.
With care we tread this life in zest,
Hoping our commitment to the moment is for the best.

The Road to the Unknown

Walking down the cobbled streets,
As we overlook the sand meeting the sea before me.
The streets are bustling with people from near and far,
But I seek the road to the unknown at any hour.

Tucked away from the hustle I yearn,
Only the sea sees my insanity in turn.
The sound of the waves from dawn to dusk is the only noise,
The quaint road to the unknown is my only choice.

The world seeks an aura different from mine,
My joy in equations echoes a rare line.
When material prowess has much show,
These roads to the unknown have a sublime flow.

The mind paddles through a flustered journey in there,
The heart treads life moments with care.
An occasional pause, we must find a way,
This road to the unknown will brighten the day.

Have you seen the complexity of emotions that ride the wave?
It's an odd journey, keeping my calm, this mind I must save.
The everyday chaos and demands of human expectations we see,
A hiatus from the grind into the road to the unknown will preserve
my sanity.

Defining possessions, as one revels in calling their own,
The papers document a territory, which you have sown.
Building castles in this realm of wealth, is the peace you hope,
Unmatched is the joy, in the road to the unknown, is a new scope.

The ocean and sea have no masters that claim,
To own them, by defining the boundary with their name!
Innominate as man would call them with an air of pride,
But this road to the unknown has its own universe to stride.

The forests have boundaries of their own we see,
Animals tread to places taken by mankind, oblivious but free.
Human animal conflict they say with rage,
It's the road to the unknown that is protected from enrage.

The fabric of life is delicate and nurtured with care,
The amiable glance has more power than one hopes to share.
Humanity may get lost in material wish lists I know,
But the road to the unknown of selflessness will find its glow.

Remnants of a Vision

Remnants of a vision have a new fabric to unveil,
Stirred emotions from success or a possible fail!
The soft voices of the ones we yearn,
Now opened eyes, an incomplete dream will wait its turn.

Many thoughts, a confused mind,
Remnants of a vision, it's an impossible rewind.
The little moments making it count I say,
Have now formed a veil, is it for another day?

The remnants of a vision ride with mystery for sure,
Looking for the unknown is often here.
As we yearn for hope, love and forever blends to last,
Slipping through my hands; unable to grab it fast.

With remnants of a vision, there is truth to be told,
Of opportunities and possibilities of new and old!
Every gripping chase on a still night I see,
The dream has an odd meaning that won't set me free.

As these remnants of a vision find their way,
Through the passage of my mind that echoes my say.
Images fade and now the story has changed its scene,
Am basking in this chaos, yet soaking in the serene.

The Quandary in Us

I look around and find my life gripped by the clock,
It's always timed; there is always a new knock.
Within my heart, is a girl seeking that pause,
The quandary in us within yearns for a silence without applause!

Every word that gets typed on the screen,
It transports me to a land where I yearn to be seen.
It's a world of magic in my eyes I know,
The quandary in us seeks an unconventional show.

My story is not weaved in the fabric of society that looks,
With judgement and care, I am a poem in the books.
The quandary in us spins a dimension so rare,
It's a graphic that's unseen, but crafted with care.

The mirror in front of me, speaks with hope,
The reflection reminds me that life has a lasting scope.
The quandary in us projects on the past from another year,
To live with no regrets while learning from mistakes is the mantra
to cheer.

The nostalgia seeing the photo wall rides down memory lane,
Memories of milestones travel that truly entertain!
The quandary in us yearns to rest in this time capsule,
Treading reality, this journey is tactful.

Reflections of Auld Lang Syne

In the reflections of auld lang syne, we find who we are,
The truth unfolds to be retold through stories near and far.
This beautiful past shapes our legacy of tomorrow,
So embrace your yesterday, it's worth every joy and sorrow.

In the background, the faint song plays,
The iconic Auld Lang Syne with tears it stays.
Bringing back memories of the impermanence of life,
A fleeting life gripping any friendships free from strife!

There is a familiar ring to the day,
Reflections of auld lang syne, almost a déjà vu I would say.
The quaint streets that lined the city back then,
Almost forgotten in the hustle, but time stood still; a worthy pen.

Amidst the chaos and tall skyline,
Stands this heritage bungalow, almost dilapidated from a different timeline!
Sitting on the porch, on a rocking chair, musing over echoes of yesterday,
A graceful golden ager, almost fossilized some would say.

The decrepit walls, adorned by photos, gave a peek into another time,
Celebrations of a different freedom and a unique family chime!

She smiled with the reflections of auld lang syne reliving every photo feeling good,
For me the onlooker, in that moment, going back in time, I just stood.

There were stories of freedom that were fought with struggle for all,
It was a time, when humanity defined geography and race with appal.
The reflections of another time gone by remind us with a heavy heart,
There was a substantial price to pay for our freedom from the start.

The times were simple, lined with joy,
Gadget free games in the backyard without a fancy toy.
Shrieking excitement and pure fun for sure,
This reflection of yesteryears has an echo of innocent cheer.

Remembering the dried Oriental plane leaf from a friend's holiday stored with care,
Thoughtfully gifted in a decorative box that seemed so rare;
It was not worth any money that makes it precious to keep,
It's the reflections of a long time ago of an estranged friend for which I weep.

The last letter from a near one I read,
Reminded of the little time, wanting more in my head!
Some losses don't heal with time,
The reflections of auld lang syne fill my heart every time.

The reflections of auld lang syne have the depths of emotions here,
The mourning wife and mother, but no time to shed the tear!
Braved ahead to be the rock to the child in need,
An inspiration and hero for generations indeed!

The carefully crafted handmade card is prized,
Or the imperfectly perfect creative handmade gifts always surprised.
The unconditional affection attached to these memories is a true keepsake,
The reflections of auld lang syne have a bond that I don't want to break.

The reflections of auld lang syne ring an unforgettably planned meal,
For the mother to be by the not so seasoned companion with zeal!
It's not the diamond or the car that I wish with glee,
It's these moments that bring magic to eternity.

The reflection of auld lang syne is in awe of the pendulum or the loud ring of the Grandfather's clock,
Not forgetting the cheerful reminder of the cuckoo tick-tock,
Time is now smartly packed on the wrist or the phone,
Convenience has trumped but the glory of the antique is shown.

Technology now makes a fading memory line,
Gadgets have outgrown their time, new facets with a different shine.
But the reflections of another time radiate in black and white,
Crafted memories that shone on their own might!

We have come a long way without much tech in tow,
But joys were simple and didn't need the show.
Reflections of auld lang syne might seem limited to some,
But every lesson learnt has shaped our balanced outcome.

Its big houses, small families, more degrees, less sense,
More knowledge, less judgement, more quantity but life is dense.

Reflections of auld lang syne defined small wants and large hearts,
Time was not a luxury or privilege offered in parts.

Reflections of auld lang syne remind us of people of our past,
We hope for another chance to speak our heart before it's the last.
Aromas of that reminiscent past that tingle our taste buds,
An unforgettable childhood soaked in lip smacking food with
clothes soiled in mud.

Amidst these discoveries in the refuge of an old diary's page,
Reflections of auld lang syne captured another age.
Every page that reveals its essence through time,
It's a treasure trove of memories that is truly sublime.

Every compilation had some tears or reason to smile,
Each adventure was worth every mile.
The magical encounter, captured in a book now weathered,
Memories will remain in the life space forever remembered.

Standing in front of the mirror we see,
Three generations of us, passing on a piece of history
What came to me from my mother was a legacy so rare?
As a reflection of auld lang syne, the next generation will find it a
forgotten fare.

Memories have been built in the sands of time,
Making the moment count in this tapestry of life is a worthy rhyme.
The reflections of auld lang syne may fade with time,
But glowing in our hearts, it will always be an indelible rhyme.

It's a Pause Not the End

It's a semi colon; not a full stop

Deep in the heart, much was hidden I know,
The losses of loved ones, I was unable to let go.
Life went on, swiped to the next phase we saw,
I was told I had not mourned enough, moving on with no option
to withdraw.

A medical lapse did change everything for me,
A small injection felt like suffering till eternity.
An apology seemed so easy for them to say,
The torture and helplessness was my own life play.

It was not just the body that was broken,
The mind had reached its darkness, nothing comforting could be
spoken.
The unclear medical advice, the beeps in the OT had scarred,
Changing medications and groaning patients is the trauma on the
memory card.

The fear in the eyes of my loved one, unsure of my journey ahead,
Almost being an absent mother to my kids had wound my head.
I had seen confusion in my toddlers' eyes,
Had I broken her before building a self-defining individual, the
heart cries.

I silently looked down and hoped to be free,
It was an undeniable feeling, almost filled with lost glee.
It was oddly scary to think I felt this cheer,
Of ending it all, as the heart was not here.

That sinking feeling and loss to every emotion I know,
It's a gripping sadness, disconnected from all, hard to show.
In a world of pretence, the facade bears the smile,
But the mind and heart are away by many a mile.

The free fall gave that escape I yearn,
It stayed with me at every moment on the balcony in turn.
The pain and helplessness had taken every ounce of fight I had,
Giving up seemed like the only answer to my heart so sad!

Something with my children shook me up,
I realised the reset was needed and not give up.
Losing myself to the unknown was not an option here,
I had to start a conversation with myself and seek my own cure.

The mind saw the fight as worthy of care,
It needed my might and all the help in my share.
Ending it all seemed like the perfect escape I thought,
The depth of the struggle is beyond anything we are taught.

It's not a weak person, who chooses this route,
It's the helplessness of the mind and body that finds a respite in
this dispute.
The timely help, ears to listen without advice and judgement,
A mammoth task for the human temperament!

I am now braver to smile,
Sailing life with an evolved perspective at every mile!
I am strong but dependant on my emotions for sure,
Not regretful for the choices I make, which I must adhere.

I am a dreamer of relationships, traveller by heart.
I seize time for myself and am never guilty of this life chart.
Tears have kept me real; laughter gives me the high,
Learning from my yesterday and looking forward to life without
a sigh.

This is not a story of surviving through having nothing in the hand,
Instead it's the struggle of staying on the surface when the mind
drowns in nothingness to understand.
For some, being on the edge, this struggle is trivial and odd,
But to step back was worth defining without feeling flawed.

The Legacy to Go Forward

A life well lived, fortune has been gathered with pride,
It's a fortunate life and a worthy ride.
The legacy of this wealth will pass to these children someday,
A legal Will has these thoughts at play.

Bloodline or heirloom is the known legacy to pass,
From one generation to another, it's another class.
Material possessions seems like the top of the popularity chart,
But traditions and the family code are where I believe they should start.

Hard work and struggle are part of life one will see,
Coping with tragedy and loving the family are the foundation to this value tree.
Entrepreneurial streaks should be explained with persistence and luck there,
Marriage advice and parenting formula is a legacy worth the share.

Fortune will be made from a life they make,
The legacy I pass is the character at stake.
We hope to inspire and shape them with traits that define a worthy life,
A strong core sprinkled with values, free from strife.

A world founded on equations that matter,
Keeping them together safe from trivial shatter.
The legacy of these bonds I pass with care,
May they nurture with love and value this life so rare

In this chaos of the daily grind,
One often forgets the joy of self-love and a true unwind.
The legacy of gifting joys and small moments to one and all,
Is what I hope to pass however big or small.

The depth of the past is the learning we yearn,
Living in the present from this learning is what we earn.
Building a future of everything that matters with care,
This blend of past, present, future is the legacy we share.

Before I Let Go

Standing at the door, I watched my dad lay in bed,
So many questions, and so much to be said;
There was no hope, is what we were told,
It couldn't have been his time to go, as the young I thought he wasn't old.

Time and events teach you to hold your own,
Be the anchor and refuse to be torn.
Before I let go, I hoped to speak my heart,
It was a time, when my life was about to start.

In a few hours so much changed for all there,
Emotions had bound us with confusion and scare.
The pause is now an unsaid truth to remain,
Until I see him with me again.

A sudden loss of another loved one I know,
It was heart gripping in every way from head to toe.
We froze, as we had no time to prepare for this goodbye,
It was an odd act of destiny, with no reason to go by.

I saw him lay there being watched by all,
My heart screamed an almost twin to me to call.
I held on to every memory that could hold my mind,
Before I let go, all I wanted was a rewind.

Always in our conversation and heart we know,
Facing life with grace, we prepare for the life show.
Everyone hoped we mourned enough, before I let go,
But sailing in our emotion, it's an eternal flow.

These losses were forced by destiny I see,
But the forgotten friend or the human heartbreaks breaks every guarantee.
Change is inevitable they say,
Moving ahead, our tears have the price to pay.

Before I let go of the friendship that didn't last,
I will look back at the happy times of the past.
Before I let go of the equations that pull me down,
Instead nurture the ones that bring happiness around.

So before I let go, with gratitude I share,
For every memory and learning with care.
Before I let go, I yearn for the strength to cope,
With life and it's unfortunate surprises, an unusual scope.

My Word - I Can

I can laugh or cry, yet be strong,
I may be right, or learn from my wrong.
I can love with all my heart,
I can bid goodbye from my life chart.

I can dream about the impossible, with cheer,
I can hope for the best, but land with a tear.
I can celebrate the small joys that the world doesn't understand,
I can choose to isolate myself for my own logical stand.

I can express myself on any platform and not fear the judgement,
The off-beat dance or the shrill to hold a note, it's my own temperament.
I can clock those steps to ace the weight goal,
Or binge into the comfort food, ignoring the troll.

I can have an opinion or choose my own silence,
I can choose my spirituality, but have my own religious stance.
I can have days of chaos, where I may not be calm,
I can be a diva or dame; it's going to be my own charm.

I can hear, when my heart listens to you,
I can choose to block the thoughts that are not true.
I can choose my skill and be defined only by my effort,
I can be the career baron or juggle as the talented home expert.

I can have a mind-set from another time,
Or be the trending one to match your rhyme.
I can laugh at myself and not feel shy,
I can accept my wrong with confidence in my eye.

I can drive any vehicle I please,
Or walk the streets with every ounce of ease.
I can be clad in the street binge that I picked,
My image will be my own life script.

I can take my 'me time' with ease,
Comments or judgements will not be my tease.
I am my own judge, I will sail my own destiny,
Walk with me if you agree to accept me till eternity.

Spice of Life

The aromas are strong; I am drawn to the bustling kitchen,
The flavours are many, the spices are hidden.
Tingling my taste buds I yearn to savour,
Just like the spice of life, there is so much flavour.

An acronym often missed, SPICES is here,
Together it nurtures the human equilibrium with cheer.
Social, Physical, Intellectual, Creative, Emotional and Spiritual
(SPICES) is the mantra to care,
With the flavours of life it's a perfect fare.

Staying connected is the Social formula to find,
Physical health is a constant remind.
Intellectual stimulation engages with more,
Creative facets touch the core.

Emotionally engaging shapes a healthy mind,
While Spiritual connection has a rare find.
As we combine these elements to balance our Earth time,
The mixed flavours infused make it a complete rhyme.

With the sweet memories and equations we make,
Tender and delicate with love, so much at stake;
Aspired by all, sweetness is a must,
This spice of life harbours trust.

A little tease, the salty twist,
Balances with fun, must on the list.
A spice of life preserves from fade,
Cherish the endurance, the best has stayed.

Life must have all flavours they say,
It's hard to leave bitterness out of the way.
There will be challenges and hurdles in life,
It's always a rollercoaster, not free from strife.

Complex and full, sour is a facet we know,
It's the result of sweetness but appears much later in the show.
It sounds complex as often regret follows to ache,
A spice of life, which we cannot forsake!

A flavour so popular, pungent for sure,
The spice and heat, heals the system clear.
As a powerful spice of life, that evokes jealousy and rage,
It's a hot emotion, we must balance and engage.

The lesser known to most, astringent is a spice we see,
It's a power sensation and nature's miracle for the body.
But in life astringent people should steer away,
Their toxicity is best avoided any day.

For most, life is viewed black and white we see,
The variance in these flavours and balance is a different path for
everyone to eternity.
Forgetting the self is often done with ease,
Remember life dishes out chances, grab it please.